How to Make and Fly

Stunt Kites

Jeremy Boyce

p

This is a Parragon Publishing Book
This edition published in 2002

Parragon Publishing
Queen Street House
4 Queen Street
Bath BA1 1HE, UK

ISBN 0-75258-799-4

Produced by Haldane Mason, London

Printed in China

Contents

Introduction

For centuries the only type of kite

you could get was a single string

kite, what you would recognize

today as a diamond or box kite, that simply went up

and stayed there. It is not certain when anyone first thought of

making a manoeuvrable kite, but it wasn't

until this century that the first

important steps were taken.

INTRODUCTION

This book aims to help you get the best out of your kite as quickly as possible. Stunt/sport kite flying is fun and it is actually very easy to learn – a bit like riding a bike. For anyone who thinks they can, this book helps you make sure you can!

The Author

Let me introduce myself. My name is Jeremy Boyce and from 1992 until 1997 I was involved in sport kite flying as part of the most successful competition and display sport kite team of the 1990s, *Airkraft*. Kite flying is something you can do in individual competitions and in teams, and team flying is one of the most exciting events. I've been involved in organizing festivals and competitions, I've done some stunt/sport kite teaching, I've written articles for kite magazines and run a kite business. All in all I've been able to experience and observe the fantastic innovations in kite design and flying technique that have shifted the reality of kite flying as far away from the old 'Mary Poppins' image as it is possible to get.

Of course, many people just want to fly for fun. It has often struck me that the instructions you get with your kite are good enough to get you going but, unless you live near a recognized flying site, you probably haven't got anyone to watch or advise you and help you understand how to take your kite to the limits of its capabilities. There are now a couple of really good training videos to help you understand some of the more radical manoeuvres popular today. But this is the first dedicated stunt/sport kite instruction book to appear specifically for the many thousands of people who are discovering that stunt/sport kite flying is one of the great things to do with your leisure time.

The Beginning of an Adventure

It is said that the kite was the second toy ever invented by humankind. So you can argue that the enjoyment of kites is now deeply embedded in the human psyche. You can also argue that, until recently, kites had kept the same basic design and flying qualities they were first made with. In spite of this few children or adults could resist the magic feel of the tugging line or the idea that they could control this flying object.

Mankind has been obsessed with the idea of flying for thousands of years. The kite represented one way he could physically attach himself to the concept of flying. It was inevitable that one day kites would drag themselves into the modern age and that's what has happened to stunt/sport kites particularly. You may be asking 'what makes a kite a stunt kite?' and the simple answer is 'a piece of string'. What differentiates a stunt/sport kite from a traditional kite is that the traditional kind will have one string attached, whereas the stunt kite will have two. Of course, there are all sorts of differences in design and technology, but it is the extra string, or flying line, which makes it possible to turn the kite left or right, making it fully manoeuvrable.

The fun and excitement that comes from a stunt kite is the same as that you get from bikes, skateboards, roller blades and snowboards. Once you've got the kite you can let rip with your imagination and find enjoyment in your toy far beyond what may, at first, appear to be possible. With the right kite, a couple of lessons and a lot of practice you too can be out there doing your axels, poisoned ivys and 540° flat spins! You can master precision compulsory manoeuvres, enter (and win) competitions and travel the world visiting kite festivals and competitions in amazing places.

How the Stunt Kite Developed

In the 1940s an US Navy officer, Paul Garber, devised a kind of manoeuvrable kite for use on ship to help the ship-borne gunners get some practice defending their vessel against attack by enemy planes. Up to that point the gunners had had to use clouds and sea birds as their targets but, unless you happened to shoot down a bird (actually pretty difficult from a moving ship), you had no way of telling how accurate you were. Garber's kite, manufactured with an aircraft design on the face, could be recovered after use to see how accurate (or not) the gunners were.

Nothing more happened until the 1970s when a British inventor and kite obsessive called Peter Powell hit on the idea of a manoeuvrable kite as an exciting new toy. Peter took the classic diamond shape and attached a long tail as a distinctive sky streamer. He succeeded in pioneering stunt kite flying as a new leisure pursuit. Peter's story is worth a book in itself. Suffice it to say that, after starting out selling kites from the boot of his car, and after some crucial UK television appearances on *Blue Peter*, *Tomorrow's World* and the magazine news programme *Nationwide* he became a household name and his kite sold in thousands. The stunt kite was born, capturing the imagination of the public.

It wasn't long before other people got in on the act, seeing the enormous (commercial) potential in the new toy's popularity. Another British company, called Flexifoil, invented an air foil or parachute-type of kite that was fast, highly manoeuvrable and incredibly durable. Flexifoil saw the value of tougher materials such as ripstop nylon (as used in the sails on yachts) and fibreglass frames. Flexifoil are still going today, selling vast numbers of the successful designs that launched the company and a number of different designs that reflect the ways stunt/sport kiting has developed in the twenty years since Flexifoil first appeared.

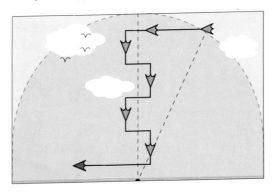

Individual compulsory manoeuvre: Square cuts

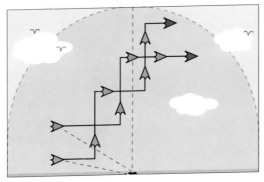

Pair compulsory precision manoeuvre: Twists

Towards the end of the 1980s, this time in America, a man called Don Tabor took his love for sailing and aeroplanes and combined the two in the delta wing stunt kite shape that is the most recognized basic design of stunt kites all over the world today. Don's kites were big, with more than a 2 m 30 cm (8 ft) wingspan, and it is size that distinguishes a stunt kite from a sport kite. A sport kite is a stunt kite that is bigger, pulls harder and is in fact more controllable than its smaller relative. Don's kites were incredibly successful and, as more people acquired them and the appropriate piloting skills, he saw the potential to turn sport kiting from simply flying around for your own amusement into a series of tests that could constitute a competitive structure. Modern sport kiting had been born.

Don laid the basis for the way sport kite competitions are run today. If you imagine the way a figure skating competition operates, with precision compulsory manoeuvres, a short routine and a long routine flown to music, you know exactly how it works in sport kiting too. And just as it is great to skate around while music plays over the loudspeakers, so it's great fun to get out in the field with your stunt/sport kite and your walkman and blast around the sky to your favourite tunes.

There is one other popular use for stunt/sport kites that we will only mention briefly in this book, since it really deserves a book of its own. It's called power kiting and it is an obvious development when you think about it. Any kite is nothing more than a sail, just like a sail on a boat, it has the potential to develop a degree of pull that can be turned into traction power. Putting it simply, the bigger the sail area of kite you can get up (by building a stack of kites or flying one extremely big one), the more pull is generated so that, in the end, the kite can pull hard enough to pull you along (scudding) or even up in

the air (jumping)! Nowadays a lot of people are getting into a new adrenaline sport called kite buggying. The pilot sits in a small three-wheeled cart and is pulled along at speed by a big (usually parafoil) kite. Like most things that are good fun, power kiting can be somewhat dangerous so consult an expert (your local kite shop, for instance) before trying it yourself.

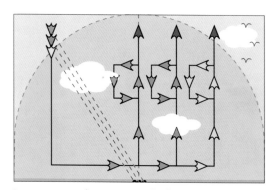

Team precision compulsory manoeuvre: Follow flank up and square

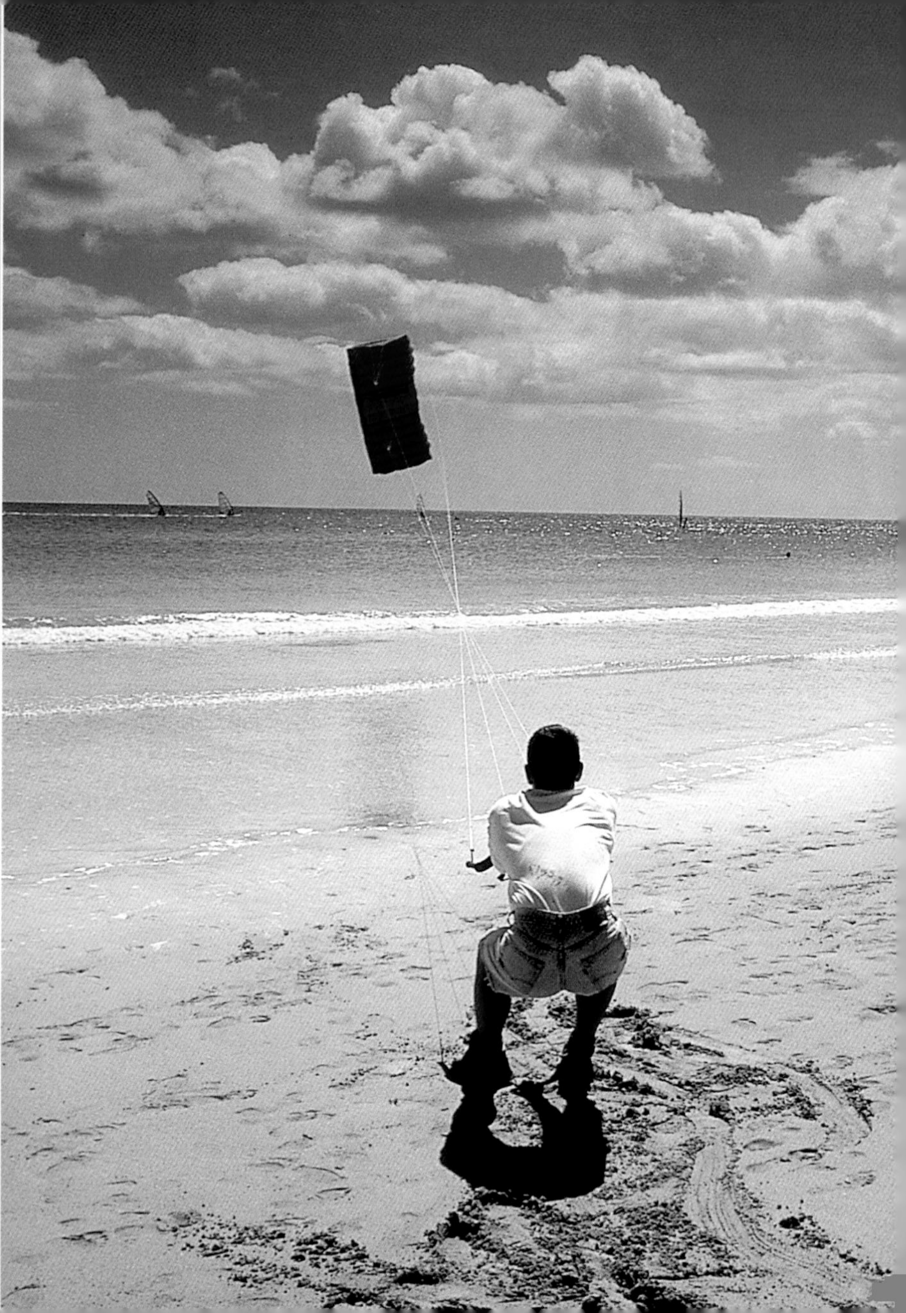

CHAPTER ONE

Preparing to Fly

In stunt kite flying, preparation can be extremely

important to the enjoyment of your day out .

Picking the right kite for your size and capabilities,

wearing the best and most comfortable clothes for flying, picking the

best possible site for your first launch and making sure that you

have brought the right extra equipment are all

discussed in this chapter.

A typical delta stunt kite. This is a scaled-down version of the big wing delta with most of the same features. Useful for learning trick manoeuvres and improving competence on leading edge take-offs and landings, this is the ideal kite for the inexperienced flier.

ESSENTIAL EQUIPMENT

There are a few things you will need to become a stunt kite flier. The first is a kite, and in general there are four types.

Entry-level Delta

Generally speaking these will be at the smaller end of the size range and, therefore, the price range. The XTRO made by Flexifoil International (*see left*) is a perfect example of this type. There are kites in this range as small as 75–100 cm (2 ft 6 in–3 ft) wingspan and they can go up to 185 cm (6 ft) in span. These would usually have a simple sail panel lay out and either a GRP (glass reinforced plastic) or protruded carbon fibre frame which should include stand offs. They come with handles and flying line included, along with a set of assembly and basic flying instructions. Not surprisingly, the bigger the kite the more it will cost and you really do get what you pay for. That is to say that bigger kites (normally) fly better and in lighter winds (meaning you can fly more often), they're more stable, they look more impressive and they pull a bit more. Most of this makes them easier to fly although, if you buy too big a kite, you may have too much pull which works against better control. Smaller kites do (usually) need stronger wind to fly so don't be surprised if you see people out flying much bigger kites on days when a small one won't get off the ground.

Big Wing/Competition Delta

With stunt kites, the bigger they are the slower they go. That's the reason why most people entering competitions would go for a big wing kite, which can be defined as 185–235 cm (6 ft–8 ft 6 in) wingspan. A slower-moving kite can be piloted more accurately (crucial for a precision competition) and is almost a prerequisite for team flying. Obviously big kites pull a lot more, but this needn't be a problem. The pull gives you essential feedback about the kite and contributes a large part of the buzz that this sport gives. It also makes kiting a very good form of exercise. A big wing stunt kite is often called a sport kite for this reason. It is possible to be more sophisticated with the design of a bigger kite so that it handles better and is more responsive. The frame and often the sail will be made from better quality materials, and being that much bigger, it'll look more impressive in the sky (this is very important if you're spending £150.00 on a state of the art kite and you expect to spend a lot of time looking at it) as will its more elaborate sail pattern/panel cut. Flexifoil's Matrix kite shows what I mean (see below). The kite should have a much wider wind range and can probably be bought in Ultra Light (very light wind) and Vented (very strong wind) versions. A vented kite has two or more of its panels replaced with gauze, allowing the wind effect to be decreased, slowing the kite down (all stunt kites go faster in stronger winds) and decreasing the pull.

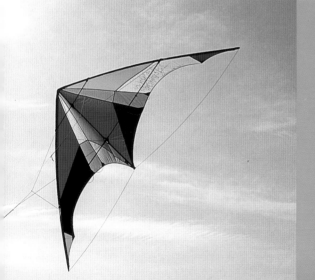

COMPETITION DELTA

The best kite for team competition, the big wing is built from state of the art materials (Icarex polyester fabric and spiral wound graphite frame) and features an anti-snag line to avoid line catches in radical manoeuvres. Although expensive to buy or build, these kites can be the most rewarding in the long run. Once you have mastered the basic trick manoeuvres, this kite will teach you the rest.

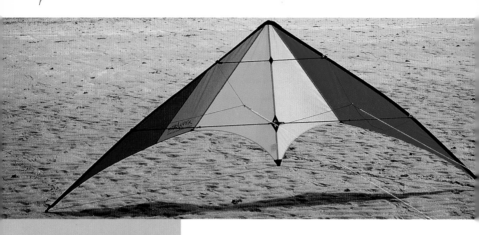

The Stranger was one of the first free-style trick kites invented. Typical of its type, it has a wide nose angle and curved leading edges and is fitted with an anti-snag line to avoid line catches during radical free-style manoeuvres.

Freestyle/Trick Delta

A couple of years ago a new trick manoeuvre was invented. It was called an axel. The kiting axel is similar in essence to the figure skating axel, making the kite flick round on its own axis in flight. The axel became the first of the new 'tricks' and it seemed to help to have a slightly different type of kite to do it with. Trick kites have a much wider nose angle and a curved leading edge. They have a deep billowed sail and a tensioned trailing edge and are fitted with anti-snag lines to stop the flying lines tangling around the tips during trick manoeuvres. Trick kites tend to be flown on much shorter flying lines making the action much faster and the kite's responses quicker. The Stranger (*see* above) is a perfect example and was one of the first trick kites on the market. Trick kites tend to be slightly smaller than big wing kites. Typically they will be around 185–210 cm (6 ft–7 ft) wingspan. Trick kites have helped make sport kiting much more accessible and exciting.

Non-delta Stunt Kites/Air Foils

Air foil stunt kites first appeared in the mid- to late 1970s and were invented by two British men, Andrew Jones and Ray Merry. Their company, Flexifoil International, makes the best known brand of air foil kite, the Flexifoil. These kites come in various wingspan sizes, are easily linked together to make big, strong pulling stacks (*see* right) and are among the most durable kites around. They are less accurate than deltas and you certainly couldn't trick fly them but they are great fun and really race around the sky. In fact the fastest recorded stunt kite is a 185 cm (6 ft) Flexifoil Stacker at over 185 kph (110 mph)! Air foils are great for traction – i.e. being pulled along. This can be either standing up or on one of the kite buggies mentioned earlier.

AIR FOILS

Five air foils in a stack might seem excessive for even the most power-hungry kiter, but the adrenalin rush is fantastic! It is this sort of set-up that can break world speed records.

OTHER ESSENTIALS

If you're buying a small kite it will probably come with handles and flying lines included. Larger kites tend to come without lines so you will need to get some. There are a number of different options for handles and lines.

Flying Lines

The choice of flying line is very important since it will need to be strong enough but of a good enough quality not to detract from the performance of the kite. After all, if you're spending over £100.00 on a good kite, you want it to fly as well as possible. There is such a thing as high quality or braided line (string), which is what you should ask for. Lower quality or twisted lines are much heavier and more stretchy, reducing the kite's performance and responsiveness. High quality lines are much lighter than low quality lines of equivalent strength and they are generally narrower, making your kite quicker and giving it a bigger field of movement since there is less drag/resistance. They are smoother, making multiple twists in your lines less likely to bind, and after a short amount of flying they lose all their stretch, giving you instant response from the kite. The ascending order of string quality is Nylon twist, Polyester braid, Dacron braid and the best, Spectra/Dyneema braid.

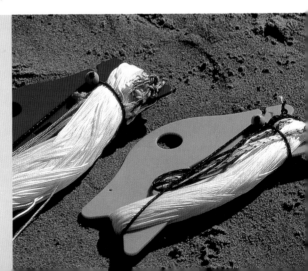

FLYING LINES

Spectra flying lines wound in pairs onto line storage winders. Spectra and Dyneema lines are a must with any decent kite. Nylon or polyester lines of the same strength could be up to four or five times thicker and heavier than the Spectra/Dyneema type.

Even then there are different qualities of Spectra and it is even possible to coat your lines with silicone to make them even more slippery. The one down side of Spectra/Dyneema is its low melting point. Because lower quality line has a higher melting point than the high quality line, people who cross your lines with the former type will invariably cut your kite down. If you want to fly together (pairs or team) you can only do it with Spectra/Dyneema as the others bind together too easily when the lines get crossed. Crossing Spectra/Dyneema with another high quality line should be fine. Spectra and Dyneema need to be sleeved at the ends because of friction. Without sleeving the line would cut through itself where you tied your knots. For the same reason, you can't just tie broken lines back together again, instead you have to splice them, and this is both time-consuming and complicated.

The other issue is line length. Around 45 m (150 ft) is considered the maximum, even for a big wing or power kite. Shorter (as well as lighter) lines can help in light winds, but shorter lines cut down your field of manoeuvre somewhat, so it is probably best to start off on a reasonably long length. With a big wing 40 m (135 ft) is a good length for individual or pair flying, but use a slightly longer length for team flying. With a trick kite less is better – 25 m (80 ft) is considered long and you'll find lots of people flying with 9–15 m (30–50 ft). In low winds line length could be reduced to 4–5 m (15 ft), but be careful – short line flying is a real reaction tester and can result in a few broken rods. Don't worry about it too much, because breaking rods usually means you're learning something. Flying line can be used to extend your kite's wind range by using very light line in lighter winds (35 or even 20 kg/80–50 lb) or heavy line in heavier winds (90 or 135 kg/200–300 lb, even up to 225 kg /500 lb for team flying in 50 kph/30+ mph).

TECHNICAL SPECIFICATIONS

The technical specifications of twisted lines (top illustration) mean that they are heavier and prone to stretch. In consequence the kite flown with twisted line will not manoeuvre well and, after a while, the lines will tend to differ in length, making control doubly difficult. The braided line (bottom illustration) is a much more satisfactory solution, in that because of its more complex structure it is less likely to stretch, it is stronger and it has a smooth profile – all qualities which aid flying. Braided lines can be bought made out of polyester, dacron or, ideally, Spectra/Dyneema.

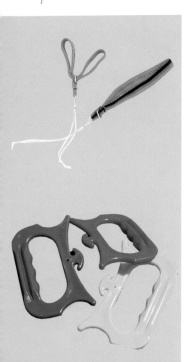

Handles

The type of plastic handles you get free with a packaged kite will be about the cheapest thing on the market, that's how the manufacturer can afford to supply them. You can (and should) get hold of some better (heavier and contoured) ones for a little more money. Cheaper handles dig into your hands more with the pull of the kite. The main alternative to plastic handles are wrist (or even finger) straps. These are fabric bands about 3 cm (1.5 in) wide sewn into a loop which you wear around your wrist (or fingers) and which attaches to your flying lines. It's a much more comfortable way to carry the pull of any kite (you can take the weight in your arms or shoulders rather than your fingers) and gives better feedback about how the kite is flying than plastic handles do. The only down side with wrist straps is that you can't (as you can with plastic handles) adjust the length of line you're flying on. That means if you want to fly on different lengths of line you need to have more than one set. With straps you also need a line winder to wind in on. The good news is that you can wind both lines simultaneously onto a modern line card winder with few or no twists. To fly big power kites you would use a padded wrist strap. An ordinary flat one would hurt with the pull of the kite. In a very light wind you might use finger straps which give a more acute control. There is a half-way stage between handles and straps – it is called the Sky Claw system, which is a cushioned handle, more comfortable to hold than plastic. Again, it is not possible to wind line onto and therefore uses another type of winder and handle holder. My own preference is for wrist and finger straps, but try some different things out and choose what you feel comfortable with.

HANDLES AND STRAPS

Soft fabric wrist and finger straps (see top) are a more comfortable way of controlling a kite than the harder and less forgiving plastic handle. If using a plastic handles try to go for the contoured, chunky ones, like those shown above, because in stronger winds the plastic ones dig into your hands.

Some More Essentials

Other essentials include a ground peg/stake of some description. When getting ready for solo launch this is used to hold down the handles while you stand the kite up before launch. You can use a tent peg or even a screwdriver.

Another good idea is an equalizer, a cunning little gadget that helps you get your flying lines to exactly equal length. Get one at your local kite store.

You'll also need a good pair of sunglasses as the chances are you're going to be spending a lot of hours looking at your kite in a strong sun. Cycling glasses are good. Not only do they look cool, but the lenses filter out ultraviolet rays brilliantly. They're also very light weight and won't slip off.

You probably need to carry a bottle of factor 20 sun cream during summer, along with a good set of waterproofs, some warm gloves and/or a fleece top for those sudden downpours. Lots of people get completely hooked and are out in all weathers. Of course, you could just emigrate somewhere hot.

And you may well want to have a personal stereo to keep yourself amused/inspired or so you can practise your competition ballet. Finally, get some cool, loose-fitting sports/leisure clothing and a good pair of trainers and you're away.

CABANA °

You may want to get hold of a field shelter (cabana or small tent) if you're spending whole days out in the field. Being cheap and easy to set up they are ideal. However, in the depths of winter (if you are that hardy) a proper tent would be more advisable.

BEFORE LIFT-OFF

Having decided on the kite you're going to fly and the kit you'll need to take, you are ready to get out into the wind and find a place to fly.

The Right Site

Finding the right site sounds easy, but you'd be amazed how many people try to fly in places where it is impossible, though with experience you'll appreciate how many places are actually quite good. To understand good and bad flying sites you need to know something about the wind. The first thing is to find an open space, away from buildings or trees. All upright obstructions give a 'wind-shadow' of turbulent, bumpy air of a length up to seven times the height of the obstruction itself – a 30 m (100 ft) tree or block of flats will give a 210 m (700 ft) wind-shadow. A hill isn't always a good place either: there can be a lot of turbulence on the downwind side.

In fact the best places to fly are usually beaches (*see* left), especially with an onshore wind coming smooth and unobstructed off

WIND

All kites fly best in a smooth wind. Obstructions like trees and buildings can adversely affect the flying of the kite. Here (right), a house obstructs the wind, which as it passes over and around the building is disrupted. The swirl of wind on the leeward side makes the kite very unstable.

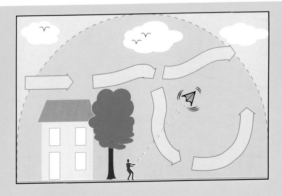

GAUGING WIND SPEED   *This table gives a broad indication of wind strength. For precise readings, wind-speed meters can be bought from kite shops.*

Beaufort	Average kilometres (miles) per hour	Effect on Environment	Which Kite?
1	2–5 (1.2–3)	Smoke just begins to move with the breeze	Ultra Light Delta
2	6–12 (3.7–7.5)	Leaves rustle slightly	Ultra Light or medium Delta
3	13–20 (8–12.5)	Small branches sway and smoke begins to move horizontally	Most kites fly well
4	21–30 (13–18.6)	Loose surface dust or sand is stirred and larger branches sway	Large kites will begin to pull
5	31–40 (19.3–25)	Surface waves begin to form on water	Good buggy conditions
6	41–50 (25.5–31)	Trees begin to bend with the force of the wind	Excellent for buggies, power kites, vented kites

hundreds of miles of open sea. Offshore breezes can be more difficult, especially if the beach has cliffs or buildings behind it. Beaches have lots of space so you can fly safely away from other people and not worry about hitting anything or anyone. And if you hit the ground you'll have a softer crash. Which brings us to inland sites. Almost any inland site will have bumpier wind. Even so, you can still get a good fly. There are some big parks, playing fields, common ground and areas of moorland where you can find good, smooth wind. My own local field comprises 85 soccer pitches, so all I've got to do is dodge the 1,870 players to benefit from the smooth wind!

How much wind do you need to be able to fly? That depends on the type of kite you've got. Also on the quality and weight of your lines. The size of kite dictates a lot. All kites have a minimum and maximum recommended wind strength. Generally, bigger kites fly in lighter winds. Most kites become more exciting and challenging in stronger winds. However, if you hit the ground in strong wind your kite will crash hard,

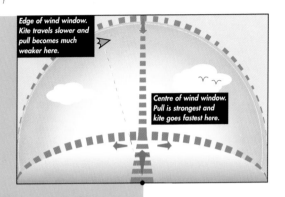

Edge of wind window. Kite travels slower and pull becomes much weaker here.

Centre of wind window. Pull is strongest and kite goes fastest here.

increasing your chances of breaking a rod. It is a common mistake to think that the best wind to fly in is when the trees are bent double. That's too much. You'll be safer, under more control and find it much, much easier (especially while you are still learning) in a moderate wind of around 10–25 kph (8–15 mph).

WIND WINDOW

Understanding the wind window/envelope can really help your flying. It will help you decide what manoeuvres you can do, where and when. The wind window dictates where the kite speeds up and when it slows down. Some manoeuvres work best going away from the 'power zone' and some moving back towards it. Some kites have a bigger wind window, or field of manoeuvre than others.

If your kite is relatively small (100–150 cm/3–5 ft) it will probably need 15–18 kph (10–12 mph) of wind to fly. A 185 cm (6 ft) kite will fly in 10–15 kph (7–8 mph) and a big wing in around 8–10 kph (5–6 mph). Super ultra light kites can fly down to 3 kmh (1 mph) or even less, but their upper wind limit is also a lot lower as the light materials used simply couldn't take the stress of anything approaching a strong wind. There's generally a wind speed indication on the television weather forecast every day, but page 21 you'll find a chart to help you work it out for yourself.

Understanding the shape and working of the wind window will also help. The wind window is the field of movement your kite has and is always the same shape no matter the type of kite or the wind strength (see diagram above). You are flying in a quarter of a sphere. The ground line (or just above it) in the centre of the window is where the wind effect on your kite is strongest, where the kite will pull hardest and go fastest. The further you fly towards the edges of the window, the weaker pull and forward movement become – if you fly too far towards the edge the kite will stall and fall out of the sky (at the top edge it will simply go to a hover position). When flying on the edges you need bigger but less aggressive hand movements.

Putting the Kite Together

All delta wing stunt kites have the same basic configuration. When you get your kite out it should be very nearly fully assembled and have instructions for the rest of the assembly process. Have a look at the diagram (see below) to familiarize yourself with the different parts of your kite.

The names of most parts of the kite describe exactly what they are or do i.e. the nose, the tail, cross spreaders, stand offs, the bridle etc. A small kite is very easy to put together because you'll have very little to put in place before you're ready to go. With a larger kite you may find that the leading edges (see diagram) are in two pieces and need to be assembled first. This should be straightforward. There will be a connector attached to one half of the leading edge and you should slide the other half into it. You won't be able to see this happen inside the fabric pocket, but you can feel what to do with your fingers. The spreader rods can now go in, and should be pushed as far into the fittings on the leading edges as they will go before putting the other end in the centre moulding. Be careful that you don't slip and poke a hole in the sail. Make sure

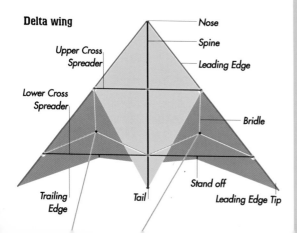

Delta wing

Nose
Spine
Upper Cross Spreader
Leading Edge
Lower Cross Spreader
Bridle
Trailing Edge
Tail
Stand off
Leading Edge Tip

the bunji/elastic cords at the leading edge tip are hooked into their mouldings. Trick kites may also come with a leech line (which tensions the trailing edge of the sail) needing to be hooked into the tip moulding. Attach the stand offs to the cross spreaders using whatever system the kite is fitted with. Check that the bridle (the harness you attach your lines to) is not snagged behind any of the other frame parts as this will seriously affect the flying. Assemble the kite once indoors before you try it out in the field. With an air foil kite there is little or no assembly required.

LAUNCHING

Most delta wing kites can be launched without a helper. If using a helper make sure they don't 'throw' the kite up into the sky as this can make for an unstable launch. Check your body position before you start. Hands should be out in front of you, ready to take a sharp pull, and you should be able to take several quick paces backwards.

LARK'S HEAD KNOT

Below; the Lark's head knot is used to attach lines to spars and bridles.

Setting Up for a Launch

After gauging which way the wind is blowing you should stake the handles/straps to the ground and, taking your kite with you, unwind the lines straight downwind. When you reach the end you can do a quick test to see if the lines are of equal length. This is vitally important for good flying and can be done by eye, which is fine, but using an equalizer is infinitely more accurate. New Spectra/Dyneema often stretches so, even if the lines start out at equal lengths, you will need to check them again.

Now you can attach the kite to the lines. Lie the kite face down, nose pointing upwind. Most kites have a simple bridle extension with a knot to tie on to. Attach the loop on the end of your flying line using the 'lark's head knot' as shown in the diagram left. Next, stand the kite up on its tips with the lines pulled tight and the kite leaning back about 35° from vertical. It won't take off until it comes upright, which you can now control from the other end of the lines with your straps/handles.

To get the kite flying smoothly, especially with a smaller kite, you will need to get it 5 m (20 ft) off the ground quite quickly, which requires a sharp pull with your hands and arms along with several steps backwards, either walking or running. So, making sure the space behind you is clear, stand ready to take a large step backwards, but lean slightly forward with your hands/arms out in front of you at around chest height. Now, as soon as you're sure there's (enough) wind blowing past you and towards the kite you can launch. 'Snap' your hands back quickly until they're next to your waist at either side of your body. At the same time take five or six big steps backwards and concentrate on pulling as evenly as possible on the lines. This should take the kite off the ground in a straight line and, if your set-up was good, up the middle of the wind window. If someone is helping you by holding and launching the kite, the same instructions apply except that you'll need to call to them to let go. The helper should try and avoid throwing the kite upwards as this seldom works properly. Rather, you should pull/launch the kite out of their hands.

With an air foil type kite you launch with a much smoother action, pulling the kite by walking slowly backwards and keeping the arms extended until the kite is off the ground. Avoid the kind of sudden snap you use to launch a delta wing as this tends to pull the front of the foil into the ground and prevents wind getting in through the front opening to inflate the kite.

FLYING POSITIONS

Keep your hands close together, just in front of your stomach/chest. Try to avoid swimming, moving your hands above your head or too far apart (as shown below). If you want your kite to climb, walk backwards rather than lift your hands.

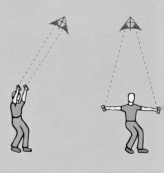

CHAPTER TWO

Flying the kite

As your kite leaves the ground and you feel

the pull increase, you're ready to take control

and steer the kite around the sky.

It is at this moment that the

excitement really begins!

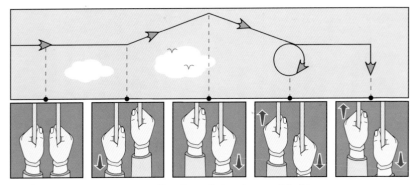

To achieve crisp square corners you will need to really 'snap' your push/pull turn.

AFTER TAKE-OFF

The kite takes off. Move your hands in front of your chest/stomach and about 20–25 cm (9–10 in) apart. The kite goes up the middle of the wind window and as it passes the 45˚ angle you can start to experiment with left and right turns and get used to the feel of the kite. To begin with pull a little on the right line. My good friend Dodd Gross devised a system that really works for describing the amount of hand movement for making different kinds of turn and I've borrowed his idea here.

Gross's system assumes five basic hand positions using both pull and push movements. For now we just want a half pull with the right, enough to make the kite track towards the right edge of the window. Before the kite gets to the edge you can turn it and go back the way you came by making a half pull on the left line. Repeat this a few times until you feel confident about it. In fact it is possible to make the kite do a turn to the right by PUSHING with the left line and *vice versa*. Try the movements as you're reading this book and you'll see what I mean. It has the same effect, but achieves it in a different way. Try it with the kite and get used to the idea because push turn is a concept that will help enormously later on.

Now it's time to start looking at full loops. A full loop is started the same way as half turn so begin by pulling the right line (to do a right loop) and increasing to a full pull so that the kite turns to the right and keeps going in a circle. As soon as it's pointing up again bring your hands back to the neutral position so

Flying an Infinity means you can keep doing right and left loops without fully crossing your lines.

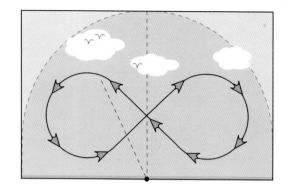

the kite continues straight up. Lines crossed over? No problem. The kite will still fly with 5 or 10 crosses (or wraps) in and all you have to do to unwrap is execute a loop to the left by reversing what you did to do the right loop.

You'll actually find that you get a much smoother turn by doing a combined pull/push turn, so to do a right loop do a half pull with the right and a half push with the left. It is a bit like steering a bike where you can't pull one handle without pushing the other.

If you get into a series of right and left loops you're in a pattern of continuous movement and can carry on flying for an infinite amount of time without stopping. This pattern is actually called Infinity (after the mathematical symbol) and if you can get to grips with a basic infinity you're ready to get into much more adventurous stuff. First of all try to expand your infinity gradually so that it goes out towards the edge and down quite low in the turn, before flying a nice big long diagonal.

If you can fly endlessly the next important thing you need to know is how to stop. There's a simple way to do this. Fly towards the edge of the window and as the kite begins to move slower and pull less steer it down towards the ground. Soon it will completely stall and fall gently to the ground. We'll look at a standing up landing later. When you are flying, if you think the kite's going to crash try and resist the urge to pull on the lines to recover it. Instead, throw your arms forward or even run towards the kite and it will crash more gently. Pulling accelerates the kite into the ground, making a break more likely. Try to avoid lifting your hands above your head when you're flying. This doesn't make the kite climb, pulling and/or walking back does that.

Remember, when you are practising any manoeuvre, to try and practise things on both sides of the window so you don't become 'one-sided'.

ADVANCED TECHNIQUES

Following are the techniques and tricks which make sport kiting such an absorbing and exciting sport. Be warned, however, that only practice makes perfect and you should be prepared to spend many hours in cold places honing the likes of snap stalls and under axels.

Speed Control

The first technique is called speed control. As you'll soon find out, a kite slows down as it climbs, accelerates when you pull/walk backwards, speeds up when flying downwards and decelerates as you walk/run forwards. Speed control can be important in a precision figure where the consistent speed of the kite is a scoring factor and is vital in team or pair flying where you have kites moving in opposite directions. Also you can expand your wind window left and right by walking in either direction. In fact speed control can really add to what you do with your kite and is integral to some of the best tricks.

Flying Geometric Shapes

Start off by flying a horizontal pass about 15% of the way up the window. The way to get into the pass is to not quite finish one of the loops of your infinity, say the left one. As you come down the left hand side try to come out pointing across the window instead of up (the diagram above right shows what I mean).

GROUND PASSES

Horizontal passes just above the ground can be very exciting. See how low and steady you can make them. You will need to keep one hand above the other and reverse your hand positions to make passes in the other direction.

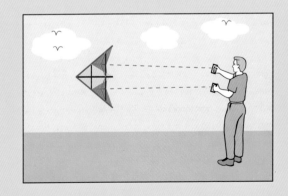

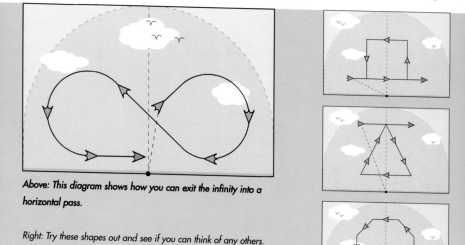

Above: This diagram shows how you can exit the infinity into a horizontal pass.

Right: Try these shapes out and see if you can think of any others. With practice you'll notice your turns becoming crisper, especially when you learn to use a flick of the wrist as your push.

You'll probably need to keep one hand above the other (*see illustration on opposite page*) to hold the pass. At first, try flying across the window and turning up 180° just before the edge to execute another pass in the other direction a little higher. Do another 180° turn up at the other side then after the third pass turn down 180° to do another followed by another 180° down at the end of the fourth pass and this will give you a continuous pattern of passes (a ladder) that doesn't wrap your lines.

As you fly your lowest pass (from left to right) wait until you've gone half way between the centre and the right edge and then try a half pull turn with your left hand. At the same time make a half push with your right hand. This should turn the kite through 90° to leave your kite flying straight up. The combination of push and pull gives the sharpest square corner. If you've got a noisy kite you will hear the effect as well as see it. Execute another left 90° turn to fly across the window, another to turn down (walk forwards now to slow the kite down as it flies towards the ground) and finally another to turn across on the same pass as your first one. Congratulations, you've just flown a square shape in the sky and introduced yourself to the concept of flying geometric shapes. Other shapes can be flown by using different degrees of the same turn.

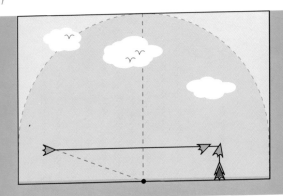

LANDING

A perfectly executed landing on the edge of the window is an elegant solution to re-launching and a stylish way of finishing a routine. From a low pass, the crisp turn and movement forward can control the trickiest stunt kite.

Below: As the kite reaches the edge of the wind window it will slow.

Landing with Style

At some point you're going to want to land the kite, if only to have a rest. We looked earlier at how to land the kite lying down on the edge of the window. Now you can learn to land with the kite standing up ready for take-off. Once again you'll need to get into a low pass manoeuvre. As the kite moves towards the edge of the window, but before it loses power, execute a square corner to turn up and as you do push your arms and take a few steps forwards and the kite should settle down on its points (*see illustration above*). Your square corner will have to be very controlled to keep the kite horizontal just above the ground. Then you can lean the kite back so it won't take off, stake your handles down and have a rest. With practice you'll be able to make this much snappier and soon you'll be able to land spectacularly in the middle of the window. A good snap landing comes from a good stall.

Stalls and Snap Stalls

You can add contrast to your flying and help set up certain tricks by performing a stall or snap stall. It is what it says, a way of stopping the kite and holding it still for a moment before doing something else. The simplest stall involves throwing both arms forward when the kite is flying straight up. If you move towards the kite afterwards you'll keep it stalled longer. A more dramatic stall can be achieved when flying horizontally. The effect is like the landing but higher off the ground. Fly your kite left to right across the window and when you're half way from the centre of the window towards the right execute a big push turn with your right hand (turning the kite upwards) followed by a half push with your left. This should stop the kite before it picks up wind and starts moving up. The faster but not necessarily bigger you can make your hand movements the snappier your stall will be – and snappier still if you can introduce a small pull with the left hand as you begin the big push turn with your right. It will take practice to get this right and keep the kite horizontal. You'll find that often the kite overbalances one way or the other. This will actually be useful when you come to the Trick Flying section later on (*see* page 40).

Stalls and snap stalls can add a different dimension to your flying. Many kites have a tendency to 'wallow' during a stall. See how well you can control the kite's horizontal pitch in a stall by adjusting your hand positions and moving forward slightly.

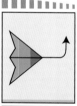

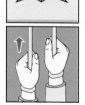

Start by flying towards the edge of the window. Begin with a small, quick pull on the left line.

As the kite begins to turn up, make a fast push with the right line. The kite now points upwards.

Finally, make a short push with the left line and balance the kite in the stall with both lines.

Here the stunt kite has not completed the full roll onto both its wing-tips before the wind catches it and sends it into the sky. Notice here that the breeze is blowing across the beach from the sea – this allows for a very smooth and predictable wind.

ESCAPES

Often you may find the kite has landed nose down (resting on its leading edge) so you've got to go and stand it up again to take off. Not so fast! There are a couple of good and easy escapes that will save you a lot of walking.

Leading Edge Take-off

This is easier with the kite facing AWAY from the centre of the window. Assuming you are near the right edge, keep your right hand steady and gradually pull on the left line until the kite looks as though it is falling towards you. At that moment pull with both hands quite hard, but with the left hand more than the right. At the same time take a few steps backwards, enough to bring the kite up off the ground and into the wind again.

To keep kite steady push with 'top' hand (left in this case).

Gradually pull the top line so that the kite starts to fall forward.

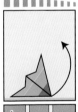

As the kite falls forward pull both lines, but the top line more.

Rollover

This is easier with the kite facing TOWARDS the centre of the window. Assuming again that you are near the right edge of the window, push your right hand forward so the kite is leaning back a little. At this point bring your right hand round anti-clockwise underneath your left hand and then across your stomach and towards your right hip. Just after you start the movement with your right hand (which brings the kite onto its other leading edge) begin an anti-clockwise circle with your left hand going towards your stomach then towards your left hip. The combined action should roll the kite round onto its tips and uses the movement of the wind towards centre window to help it along.

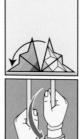

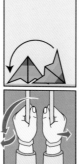

Lean the kite back slightly by pushing on the 'top' line (in this case the right).

Bring your right hand round in an anti-clockwise circle.

Almost simultaneously begin moving your left hand around and outward.

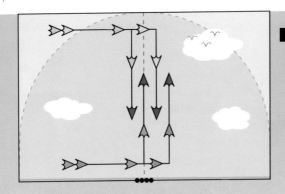

TEAM FLYING BASICS

One of the most enjoyable ways to fly (and one of the best buzzes) is team flying. This is where two or more fliers stand close on the ground and synchronize the kites into a formation to do some manoeuvre sequences. It looks great and feels twice as good as it looks, so it is definitely worth trying if you can find some people to fly with.

You'll need to have or get reasonably matched kites and lines. The kites should be matched for speed and the best kites to fly initially are definitely the big wings. They are slower and steadier-tracking and you can create faster apparent speed by flying away from or towards each other. You'll also need some matched lines. Spectra or Dyneema is a must, preferably the same length (40–45 m/130–150 ft is good) or slightly staggered and the same strength. Some people argue that you should fly one strength heavier in team than you would in individual because of the extra stresses of compound wrapping of the lines and to slow the kites slightly.

If you're going to fly with other people, first write down a sequence of manoeuvres you can try to fly and talk them through (have a look at some of the team notation in the illustrations for how to write your ideas down), agree who is going to be leader and what commands you will use and agree what to do in an emergency. A useful technique is 'stick practice' with small replica kites on the end of spare carbon rods. Stick practice will allow you to make sure what you've written down can actually be flown before you get into the sky and start breaking your lovely kites trying to do the impossible. Everyone else will think you're mad, but who cares?

Get used to flying a team infinity before trying anything else (*see below*). It is a really useful continuous pattern and what you need most to be a good team flier is lots of time in the air. To fly a good infinity you need to know a couple of things. Give yourselves a comfortable space between the kites, 15 m (50 ft) is good. Number Two flier sets the spacing and the others behind should try and match that. Flying in a straight line you should fly directly behind the next kite, aiming your nose at the centre piece. However, in a corner this changes – as the kite in front turns you should aim your kite tip at its outside wing tip and keep doing so until you come out of the turn and resume straight line flight. Aiming for the tip stops you closing in on the kite in front and maintains the comfortable spacing.

TEAM FLYING BASICS

It takes a lot of flying to get ready to be a team flier. It then takes a lot of flying together to start to feel confident as a team. Get as much air-time as you can. Don't be put off if you have crashes, it is all part of the learning process. Simply keeping the spacing during an Infinity can be a bit of a test.

TEAM INFINITY (top) Note how the following kites are aiming for the outer tip of the one in front's trailing edge. In this way they all fly the same curve and can regulate the distance apart.

HORIZONTAL THREAD AND LOOP (bottom) Each member of the four-man team executes the loop at exactly the same time.

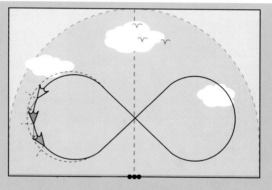

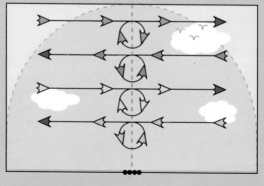

Once you've mastered infinity you can start getting into more complex stuff. You will need to use the low horizontal pass to get into manoeuvres and need to get back into infinity quickly afterwards. Whoever is calling the commands should give three commands before you start each new manoeuvre: one to describe the whole manoeuvre (e.g. 'team diamond' or 'thread'); one as a preparatory call ('ready') and one to commence the sequence ('turn' or 'break' work well). Then you'll need to give a command for every other turn in the sequence and one to go back into the infinity afterwards (most teams use 'fall in' for this).

The other thing you need is an emergency procedure (unless yours is the first team never to make a mistake) to sort yourselves out when necessary. We used to use the call 'fire drill' and at this point anyone still flying would go to the top of the window and stay still while anyone who had crashed sorted out their kite and relaunched. It is the kind of discipline that helps make learning happen more quickly.

All you need to do now is practise, practise, practise. Team flying is actually quite straightforward as long as you practise enough. You'll probably find that when you think it is going really badly, other people think it looks brilliant. You nearly always find someone watching when you fly a kite but you always get a crowd when you team fly. And get ready for lots of people asking how it is that your strings don't get tangled!

TEAM FLYING

Teams usually fly with some kind of stagger, achieved either by using different-length lines or by standing in a staggered formation on the ground. This helps avoid turbulence from the leading kite affecting those behind.

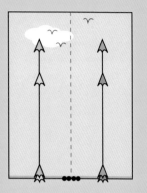

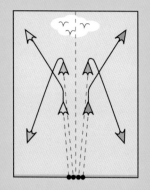

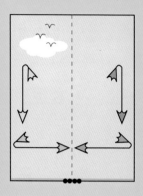

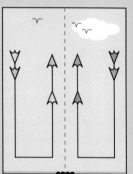

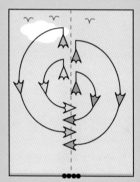

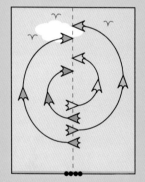

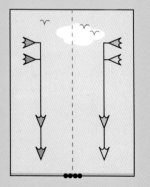

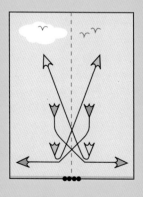

TEAM FLYING

These diagrams were taken from one of the plans used by the team I used to fly for called Airkraft. The sequences always began with simultaneous launches and then moved step-by-step through over twenty manoeuvres.

A really radical manoeuvre is an axel cascade which is a series of axels in opposite directions, each one initiated just as the kite comes out of the previous axel, but before it recovers power.

Left: The ideal setting for a kite flier's first axel. Uninterrupted sun, uninterrupted wind will help you succeed!

TRICK FLYING

In 1993–4 kite designers hit on a new style of kite that would enable a different kind of flying. It coincided with the invention of a different kind of manoeuvre, called an axel, and gave birth to a whole new style of flying called 'trick flying'. The pioneers of this style were looking for the same kind of radical performance in a kite that you could get from a BMX bike or a skate board.

The style of the kites was vastly different, with much more curved leading edges and wider nose angles. And the way the kites were flown changed too. For a start fliers chose much shorter lines, since you could get a sharper response with the kite close to you. With such a small field of manoeuvre flying became more intense, but the amount of extra things you could do was more than enough recompense. The axel, a sharp flicked spin, gave rise to other tricks: half axels, under axels, axel take -off, coin tosses, axel cascades, multiple axels, slot machines, flat spins, 540° flat spins and yo-yos. The modern flier's vocabulary bears little relation to that of even fouryears ago.

The starting point for all trick flying is the axel. You'll need an appropriate kite. A trick kite is ideal but you can do an axel with most bigger kites and some good quality lines of around 15–20 m (50–75 ft) length.

To set up for an axel fly towards the edge (the right edge) of the window about 15% up. Execute a stall/snap stall, but do it so that the kite overbalances slightly and the left tip of the kite is below the right tip, nose pointing slightly back into the window (*see illustration*). You will need to keep the kite 'floating' in its stall while you perform a double movement with your hands: first a hard pull with the right line (it is the speed of the movement or 'pop' that counts); second, but virtually simultaneously, a push with the left before bringing both hands back to the 'neutral' position while the kite completes its axel. Normally these two movements would turn the kite to the right but with the kite floating and overbalanced it flicks round in a tight (almost flat) spin to the left on its own axis. The kite must come round at least 75% of the spin before you begin to recover it from the float by pulling on both lines. This is called an over or normal axel and it'll take a bit of practice before you get it, but once you get your first one there will be no stopping you.

When you're setting up for the axel with your stall you will sometimes end up with the kite overbalanced the other way, nose pointing out of the window. At this point you could execute what is known as an under axel. If you reverse the double movement described above, so that you 'pop' the left line and push with the right, the kite will axel to the right and you can make your recovery with the kite pointing back into the window.

To overbalance the kite push forward more with your right hand.

Now execute a combined pull with the right hand and push with the left.

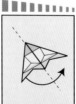

As the kite comes round 270–360° bring hands together to recover.

AXEL

The axel is a sharp, flicked spin that actually turns the kite in the opposite direction to that which you would expect. You may learn the axel quickly or maybe it will take a little time. Either way, once you get it, there will be no stopping you.

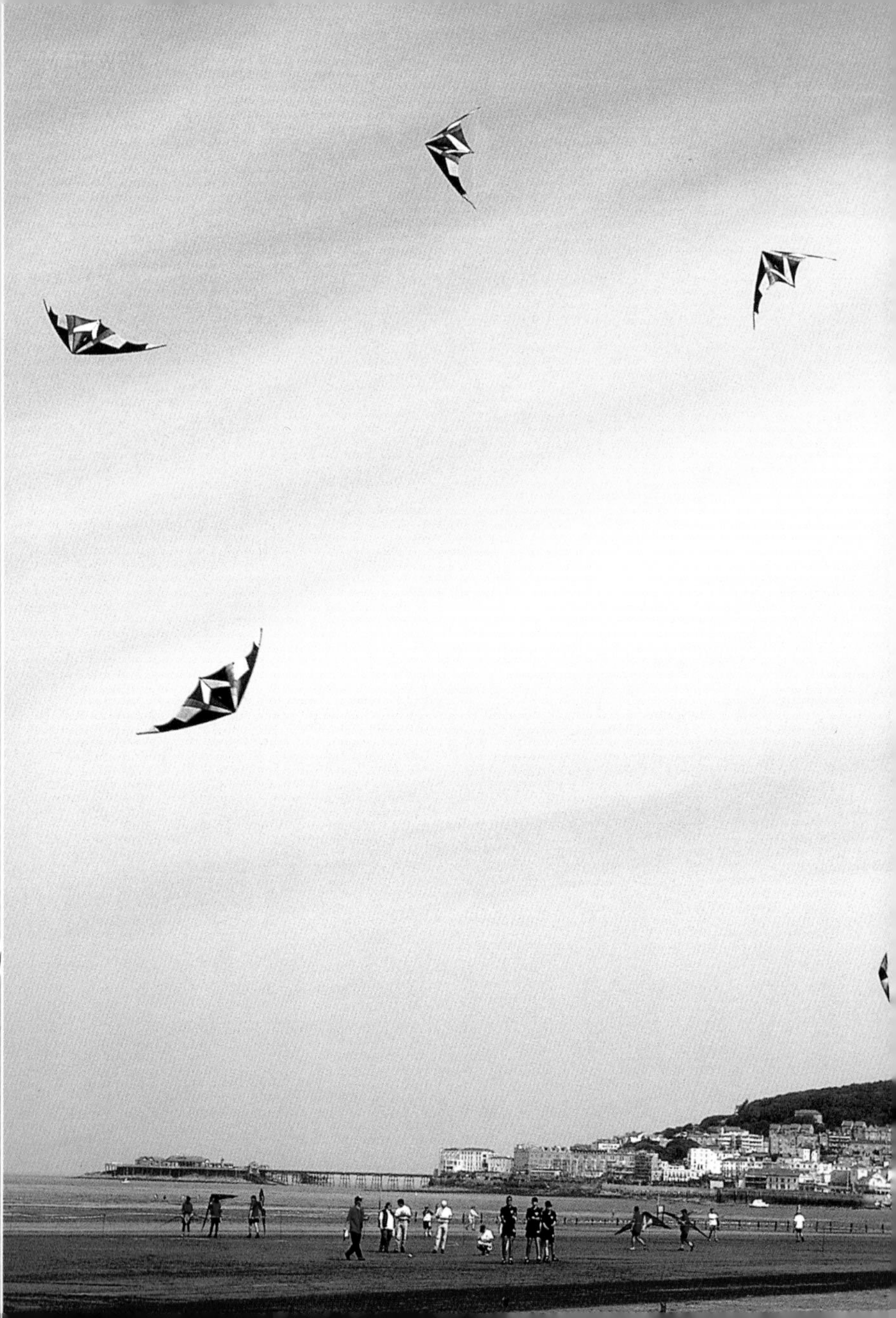

CHAPTER THREE

Manoeuvres

Following are some of the best manoeuvres for

individuals, pairs and teams.

INDIVIDUAL MANOEUVRES

THE DICE: This is a big manoeuvre requiring long, straight lines with crisp, square corners. Make sure your vertical entry and exit lines do not cross.

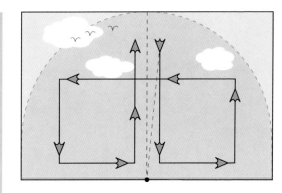

THE STAR: One of the toughest new manoeuvres. The acute turns at the points are difficult to make accurately. Hitting and holding the right line afterwards is also tricky

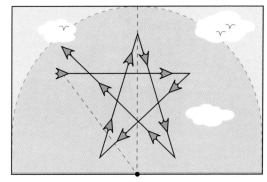

PINWHEEL: Make sure your entry line is high enough to avoid squashing the manoeuvre down the wind window. Watch out for the big intersection at the centre of the manoeuvre. Try to make all the triangles exactly equal in size.

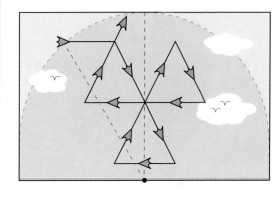

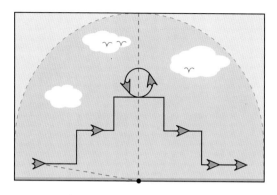

INDIVIDUAL MANOEUVRES

LADDER WITH ROLL: The trick here is to start far enough left to still have power in the kite as you exit on the left. Walking left for the entry and right for the exit will help.

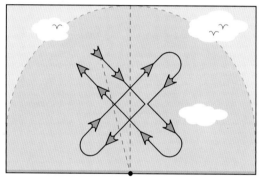

TUBULAR 'X': Hitting the correct angle on your entry is critical here. The turn at the bottom right point of the 'X' is very tricky.

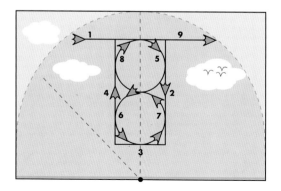

EIGHT IN A RECTANGLE: Fly the rectangle first, then concentrate on keeping the eight within the rectangle and really focus on the horizontal exit line. The eight should be two circles laid on top of one another.

PAIR MANOEUVRES

'H': The entry line must be well matched and don't get too close together at the centre. Be careful that your exit is clearly higher than your entry.

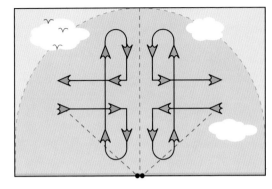

STARBURST WITH LOOPS: Check that your entry is exactly matched and that the loops are at exactly the same height. Leave a big enough space between the kites on the vertical exit.

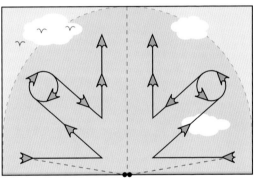

THE WIGWAMS: Speed control is vital to make sure that the kites pass in front of/behind each other properly. Exit line is higher than entry line.

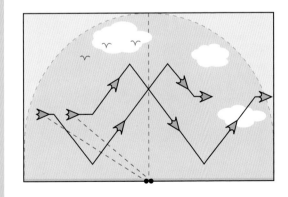

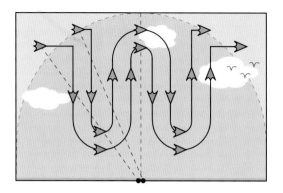

PAIR MANOEUVRES

DOUBLE 'DOUBLE U': This is a very difficult speed manoeuvre. You may well find that you are running out of wind window before you reach the exit. Entry and exit are very high in the window.

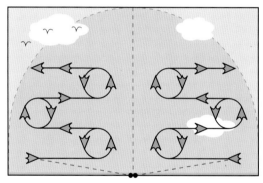

SNAKE WITH LOOPS: Match entry lines and don't come too close together at the centre. The second loop is very important for setting the entry to the third loop.

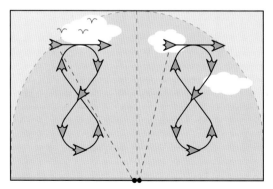

EIGHTS: Turning is the critical factor here. Try a number count as you fly the manoeuvre, starting with a one and finishing with a five as you exit.

TEAM MANOEUVRES

POWER DIVE WITH ROLL: Pay attention to the vertical lines making sure they don't cross. Watch all four kites during the roll to make sure you exit the roll simultaneously.

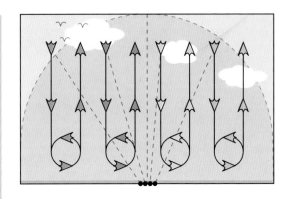

DIAGONAL LOOPS: The timing of the loops needs careful attention. Hitting the right angle for the diagonal lines is important. Exit line is quite high.

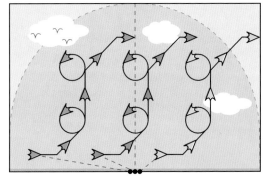

FOLLOW ROLL, ACROSS ROLL: One of the toughest. The roll on the ground pass is quite small. Controlling the speed of the kites on the higher pass before the second is difficult as the top kite has very little power and the bottom one has lots.

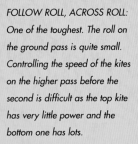

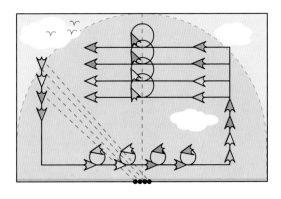

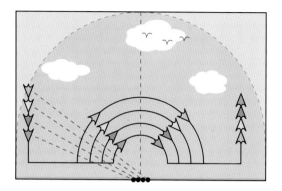

TEAM MANOEUVRES

L'ARC DE TRIOMPHE: A big speed control manoeuvre where the kite on the inside needs to travel slowly (walk forwards) and the kite on the outside needs to speed up (run back). Watch the horizontal line just before exit.

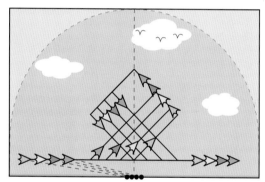

THE BASKET: Another tricky speed control manoeuvre. Also, you will need to make it acutely pointed at the top to stop it squashing down and appearing flat. Watch out for turbulence on the exit.

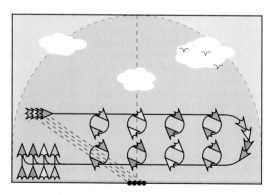

HAIR-PIN WITH LANDING: Get the loops exactly on top of/underneath each other. This means keeping the spacing as you make the turn downwards on the right. The landing is sequential, so No. 1 lands, then No. 2 flies over No. 1 and lands. The same is true of Nos. 3 and 4 as they too fly over the lower numbers.

CHAPTER FOUR

Designs

In the following pages you will find four exciting designs by kite-design guru Carl Robertshaw. The first, called 'Pump', is the ideal beginner's kite, being easy to assemble and easy to fly. 'Sushi' and 'Tranquillizer' are more complex two line stunt kites. 'Flash' is a four line kite which is easy to make but testing to fly.

Before You Start

Making your own kite from the designs which follow will require a few common materials and tools, some of which can usually be found at home, others which may need to be bought from a specialist store. Most of the other materials listed can be found at any good kite store.

To get the best out of these designs please note the following points:

•Work in a well lit, well ventilated area, where you won't be disturbed, and where you can leave your half-made kite unattended while you take a break.

•Measurements are given in Imperial and/or metric depending on the usual method of supply. For example, carbon rods which form the basic frame of a kite are measured in millimetres whereas line classification is noted in the Imperial 'pound' measurement according to the amount of pulling weight it can take. In the case of all measurements, preference is given to the metric system.

•Make sure you are familiar with the techniques described in 'General Information on Construction' (see opposite page) before starting designs 2, 3 and 4. If you are at all unsure about how to use a sewing machine or soldering iron, ask the kite shop from which you bought your raw materials or the manufacturer. Always know how a machine works before you launch into using it.

•Take great care when using knives, scissors, sewing machines and soldering irons.

•At the end of this section there is a general trouble-shooting and bridle adjustment section which will help you when you take your new kite out for the first time

BASIC EQUIPMENT
- **Soldering Iron**
- **Sewing Machine**
- **Craft Knife**
- **Scissors**
- **1 m (3 ft) ruler (preferably a metal one)**
- **Cutting surface (a woodwork bench would be ideal)**
- **Superglue**
- **Hacksaw**
- **Soft Pencils**

GENERAL INFORMATION ON CONSTRUCTION

Grain in Fabric:

Ripstop nylon/polyester has a grid in the fabric. It is important to take note of the way a panel is being cut in relation to the grain to maximize the fabric's durability. Indicated on each plan is the direction in which the grain should run.

Lark's Head Knot:

This knot is used for attaching bridles, adjustment points on the bridle and tying your fly lines.

Trick Lines:

You can fix a line from tip to tip through the tail nock. This enables you to do tricks more easily without tangling your bridle or lines on the tail or wingtips.

Rolling or Sewing a Trailing Edge

NOTE: The seam allowance for a trailing edge is usually 1.5 cm (0.5 in).

1 Fold 7 mm (0.25 in) of trailing edge over (see figure i).

2 Fold the trailing edge in again, so the cut edge is sandwiched between the two layers of fabric (see figure ii).

3 Sew a line 1–2 mm from the inside fold (see figure iii).

NOTE: The side uppermost in figure iii is usually the back of the kite and the underside the face of the kite.

Double/Roll Seam

NOTE: This method describes rolling the seam towards panel 2 and away from panel 1

1 Lay the two panels to be sewn face to face on top of one another, making sure the edges are lined up together (see figure iv).

2 Open out the two panels so they lie flat, with the seam uppermost (see figure v).

3 Starting at one end of the seam, fold the 1.5 cm (0.5 in) seam in half and tuck the cut edge under to meet with the stitch line (see figure vi)

4 Sew a line approximately 1–2 mm in from the folded edge of the rolled seam (see figure vii).

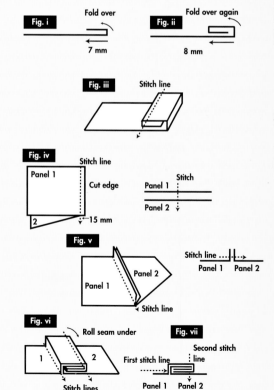

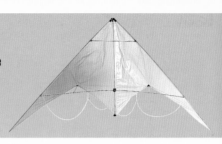

Design 1: Pump
Skill level to make: Beginner
Skill level to fly: Beginner–Intermediate
Wind range: 0–11 kph/0–7 mph
                        0–2 Beaufort scale
Cost: £5

YOU WILL NEED:

- large piece of card
- 1 m (3 ft) ruler
- permanent marker
- cutting surface
- sharp craft knife
- 2 thin strong bin bags or
  1.5 m² (1.5 yd²) 0.5 oz ripstop polyester fabric
- scissors
- clear waterproof tape
- PVC tape
- 3 x 87 cm (34.25 in) carbon rod
- 1 x 52 cm (20.5 in) spine rod
- 1 x 24 cm (9.5 in) top carbon rod
- 2 x 16 cm (6.25 in) carbon rods
- 12 x 2 mm end caps
- hacksaw
- 20 lb (9 kg) braided line
- handles

Made of lightweight bin liner or ripstop polyester, this small kite will fly in no wind. You can even fly indoors – by walking backwards you can create enough wind.

Fly on a 20 lb (9 kg) line at a length of 6.5 m (20 ft).

1 **Draw** the template out on the large sheet of thin card. Draw the outer triangle A, B, C. Along B–C mark points D, E and F. At each of the points measure at a right-angle to line B–C the stated measurement to find points D1, E1 and F1. Draw straight lines between B, D1, E1, F1 and C to make the trailing edge. Make sure you mark E1 with your permanent marker, because you will need to know its exact position later on.

2 **Cut** out the kite wing template with craft knife.

3 **Cut** each of the bin bags along the side and bottom seams so that you have two large sheets of plastic. Place one sheet on the other, making sure the plastic is smooth and then, with your permanent marker, draw around the template marking at the designated points. If you are doing this on ripstop polyester, make sure you take note of the grain as marked.

4 **Cut** around the template with craft knife and ruler, cutting through both layers of plastic at the same time. Separate both halves and stick them

together (edge to edge) down the spine with the clear tape. Reinforce the trailing edge with the clear tape all the way along both wings.

5 **At** each of the marked positions on the leading and trailing edges stick a square of PVC tape, folding it over to cover back and front of the kite sail. At the marked position on the spine at the centre joint (G) place a square front and back of the sail. Make a hole in the centre of this square in the spine.

6 **Pierce** a 2 mm end cap twice as illustrated in diagram 1.2. Slip this end cap onto the 52 cm (20.5 in) carbon rod/spine until it is 360 mm (14.25 in) down. Stick the rod, top and bottom, to the nose and tail of the kite, making sure that the end caps poke through the holes you have made in the PVC tape.

7 **Pierce** four end caps once (as per diagram 1.3). Position two end caps one on each 87 cm (34.25 in) cross spreader rod, 17 cm (6.75 in) and 58 cm (22.75 in) from the nose end of each leading edge rod, so that when you stick the leading edge of the sail to the leading

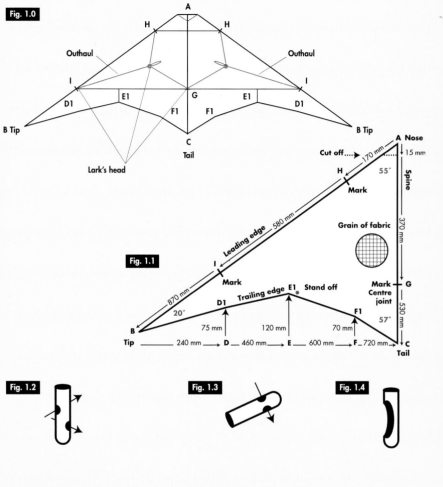

Fig. 1.0

A

H · · · H

Outhaul · · · Outhaul

I · · · I

D1 · E1 · G · E1 · D1

F1 · F1

B Tip · B Tip

C
Tail

Lark's head

Fig. 1.1

A Nose

Cut off .... 170 mm → 15 mm

H · 55° · Spine

Mark

Grain of fabric

370 mm

Leading edge 580 mm

870 mm

I

Mark · Mark
Centre
joint · G

20°

D1 · Trailing edge E1 · Stand off

75 mm · 120 mm · F1 · 530 mm

70 mm

B

Tip → 240 mm → D — 460 mm → E — 600 mm → F — 720 mm → 57°

C
Tail

Fig. 1.2

Fig. 1.3

Fig. 1.4

Fig. 1.5

Bridle

Fig. 1.6

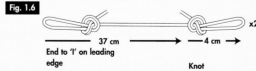

x2

← 37 cm → ← 4 cm →

End to 'I' on leading
edge

Knot

edge rod the end caps align with points H and I. Next put an end cap on the nose end of each leading edge rod. Then stick the leading edges of the sail to the rods with the clear tape, checking for the alignment of endcaps with points H and I.

8 **Reinforce** the nose and tail with PVC tape (these are the areas which get most wear and tear).

9 **Insert** the top cross spreader into the two upper leading edge end caps. Pass the bottom cross spreader through the end cap on the spine/centre joint (G). Push the two pierced end caps half way along each side of the bottom cross spreader. Put the ends of the cross spreader into the lower leading edge end caps.

10 **Cut** an oval out of an end cap as illustrated in figure 1.4. Cut a small hole in the triangle of PVC tape on the trailing edge at E1. Pass the stand off rod through the top end of the end cap you've just cut, and then through the hole in the PVC tape at E1. Push the

end of the stand off rod into the closed end of the end cap – this holds the stand off rod in place. Insert the other end of the stand off rod into the end cap on the cross spreader. Repeat this for the other side of the kite.

11 **Making the Bridle:** Cut a piece of 20 lb (9 kg) line, 124cm (148.75 in) long. Mark, with permanent marker, two points 30 cm (11.75 in) from either end. Make a lark's head knot in the middle of the line, around the spine, below the centre joint end cap (G). Next knot the other ends onto the leading edge rods (above the top cross spreader end caps at H) as illustrated in diagram 1.5. Make two outhaul bridle lines (see diagram 1.6). Using a lark's head knot attach these bridle lines to the leading edge rods just below point I or the bottom cross spreader end caps. Attach the marked pieces of line to the knots on the outhaul lines with the 4 cm (0.5 in) loops. Attach your flying lines to the 4 cm loop and the kite is ready to fly.

Design 2: Sushi

Skill level to make:
Beginner–Intermediate
Skill level to fly: Beginner–Intermediate
Wind range: 7–40 kmh/5–25 mph
2–5 Beaufort scale
Cost: £20–30

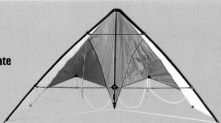

YOU WILL NEED:

- sheet of thin card
- 2 m² (2 yd²)of ripstop nylon/polyester
- sewing machine and polyester thread
- 5 cm x 3.5 m (2 in x 3.5 yd) dacron
- craft knife
- cutting surface
- soft pencil
- ruler

- soldering iron
- 4 x 6 mm leading edge fittings
- 3 x 6 mm end caps
- 3 x 6 mm arrow nocks
- 3 x 6 mm rod stoppers
- 1 x 6 mm T-piece
- 50 cm (20 in) of 3 mm cord
- 25 cm (10 in) seatbelt webbing

- 50 cm (20 in) of 3 mm bunji/elastic shock cord
- 1 x 79 cm (31 in) 6 mm carbon rod
- 2 x 128 cm (50.5 in) 6 mm carbon rod
- 2 x 64 cm (25.25 in) carbon rod
- 1 x 43.5 cm (17.125 in) carbon rod

- 2 x 17 cm (7 in) 2 mm Glass Reinforced Plastic (GRP) rod
- 2 x 25 cm (10 in) GRP rod
- 4 x 6–2mm stand off-to-sail fittings
- 2 x 2–6 mm sail-to-stand off fittings
- 100 lb (44 kg) dacron/polyester line
- superglue

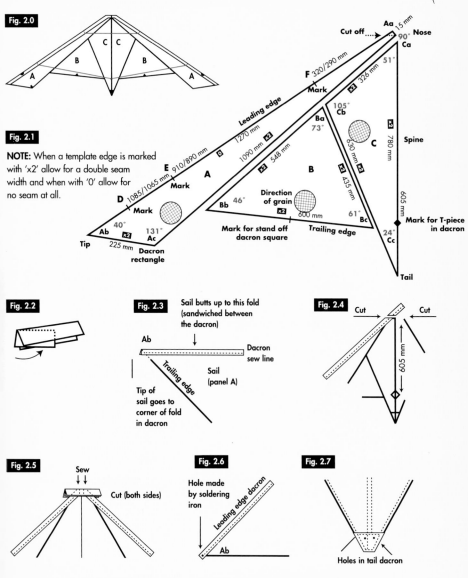

Fig. 2.0

Fig. 2.1

NOTE: When a template edge is marked with 'x2' allow for a double seam width and when with '0' allow for no seam at all.

Cut off.... Aa 15 mm
Nose
90°
Ca
51°
Cut off 326 mm x2
F 320/290 mm
Mark
Leading edge
1270 mm x2
Ba
105°
Cb
73°
630 mm x2
C
x2 780 mm
Spine
910/890 mm 0
1090 mm x2
E 548 mm x2
Mark
A
Direction of grain
B
435 mm x2
D 1085/1065 mm
Mark
Bb 46°
x2 600 mm
61° Bc
605 mm
Mark for T-piece in dacron
40°
Ab
x2
131°
Ac
Mark for stand off dacron square
Trailing edge
24° Cc
Tip 225 mm
Dacron rectangle
Tail

Fig. 2.2

Fig. 2.3
Sail butts up to this fold (sandwiched between the dacron)
Ab
Dacron sew line
Trailing edge
Sail (panel A)
Tip of sail goes to corner of fold in dacron

Fig. 2.4
Cut
Cut
605 mm

Fig. 2.5
Sew
Cut (both sides)

Fig. 2.6
Hole made by soldering iron
Leading edge dacron
Ab

Fig. 2.7
Holes in tail dacron

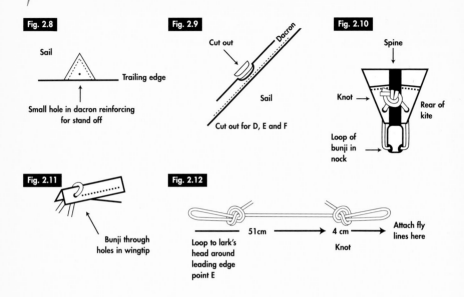

Fig. 2.8

Sail

Trailing edge

Small hole in dacron reinforcing
for stand off

Fig. 2.9

Cut out

Dacron

Sail

Cut out for D, E and F

Fig. 2.10

Spine

Knot

Rear of
kite

Loop of
bunji in
nock

Fig. 2.11

Bunji through
holes in wingtip

Fig. 2.12

51cm

4 cm

Attach fly
lines here

Loop to lark's
head around
leading edge
point E

Knot

This is a 3–4 team kite designed for a wide wind range, to be easy for the beginner but still capable of doing a wide range of tricks e.g. fast axels, flick flacks, coin tosses and side slides. The kite's flight performance is rock steady, with fast turns and stable stalls, making it easy to land, leading edge take off and fly accurate corners. This kite doesn't have much pull because of its smaller size and it also requires small hand movements to fly. To make a full size (230 cm/8 ft wingspan) kite with more pull and team capability, multiply every measurement by 1.29.

Fly on 80 lb (36 kg)/33 m (100 ft) line for three-quarters 'Sushi' and 150–200 lb (65–90 kg)/33–45 m (100–150 ft) line for the full-sized version.

1 **Copy** out the templates using the measurements given in figure 2.1 onto the thin card, adding the required seam width (usually 1.5 cm) where applicable. Cut out each panel, making sure you have noted the marks for leading edge fittings, centre piece and stand off, and especially grain direction.

2 **Cut** out two panels from each template, taking careful note of grain direction. Place the template over the ripstop nylon/polyester, draw around with a soft pencil, then cut out with the craft knife.

3 **Sew** a roll seam on the trailing edge (Bb–Bc) of panel B. Roll seam panel B to C, then roll seam panel A to B/C, rolling the seam towards panel A. Also roll the bottom edge of panel A (Ab–Ac) and sew. Repeat for the other wing.

4 **Sew** both halves together with a roll seam down the spine. Then sew one continuous additional line around the entire trailing edge.

5 **Cut** out eight squares of dacron 5 cm x 5 cm (2 in x 2 in) and fold two in half diagonally. Sew the two diagonally folded squares of dacron to the stand off points on edge Bb–Bc, so that the sail is sandwiched between each triangle. Sew two more squares of dacron (one front, one back of the sail) to the spine T-piece position (between Ca–Cc). Fold two more dacron squares lengthwise, then crosswise and sew onto the dacron rectangular corner to make a pocket for the wing tensioner at point Ac. Sew the remaining two dacron squares to the front and back of the spine tail (Cc) and cut off the excess to make a neat angle following the line of the tail.

6 **Cut** a length of dacron 132 cm (51 in) long and fold in half lengthwise. Then fold back 4 cm at one end as shown in diagram 2.2. Sandwich the sail tip between the folded-back end of dacron. Butt the edge of the ripstop up to the fold in the dacron (see figure 2.3) and start sewing the sail 5 mm from the edge (closest to the sail), making sure the tip starts at the end of the dacron strip. Sew all the way up the leading edge, making sure the ripstop fabric is butted up to the fold in the dacron all the way along. Cut the excess dacron off the nose, 605 mm (23.75 in) from the T-piece as shown in diagram 2.4. Repeat this step to produce two reinforced leading edges.

7 **Cut** 25 cm (10 in) of dacron and fold in half lengthwise. Open the dacron and flatten. Take dacron and put it on top of 25 cm (10 in) webbing. Sew the dacron to the webbing directly along the fold. Fold the webbing (with the dacron inside) in half along the new seam and place over the nose end of the kite. Sew in position as in figure 2.5. Cut off the excess webbing.

8 **Using** a hot soldering iron, seal the edges you cut in step 7 and those cut in the tail at step 5. With the soldering iron make a hole in the dacron at each tip, 3 cm (1.25 in) from the end (see figure 2.6). Then make two holes in the tail dacron (see figure 2.7). Make a small hole in each of the two stand off reinforcements (see figure 2.8). Make three cuts on each leading edge at positions D, E and F (for the shape see figure 2.9).

9 **Decide** which is to be the face of the kite and which is to be the back (usually the side the seams are to be rolled onto). Take the spine rod (79 cm/31 in x 6 mm carbon rod) and the 6 mm T-piece. Fix the T-piece to the

spine 605 mm (23.75 in) from one end. This end will become the nose end of the spine. Fit a 6 mm end cap to the nose end of the spine and insert it into the central pocket in the nose webbing. Fit a 6 mm arrow nock to the other end of the spine rod. This attaches to the tail with bunji. Cut 15 cm (6 in) bunji and pass both ends through the tail holes on the face of the kite. Tie the bunji together on the rear of the kite. Fit the spine under the knot as illustrated in figure 2.10. Cut the remaining bunji in half, giving lengths of 17.5 cm (7 in) approximately. Thread one through the holes at the wing tip, as illustrated in figure 2.11, and tie the ends together. Tuck the tails of the bunji into the leading edge when you have adjusted the wing tip bunji to the right tension – i. e. tight. Insert the leading edge rods into the dacron leading edge sleeves starting at the wingtips. Except for leading edge hole D put the leading edge fittings on as you pass the leading edge rod through the dacron sleeve. When you put the connectors on for the last of the leading edge holes, or F, also put a 6 mm cap end-on the top end of the rod before it goes into the nose. Then when the leading edge rod is in place put a 6 mm nock on the tip end (at Ab) and adjust the bunji loop to keep the rod in place. Fit a 2 mm end cap to one end of each of the 17 cm (7 in) GRP rods and a 2–6 mm stand off fitting to the other ends. Use this to tension the wing between D and Ac. With the remaining 2 pieces of 25 cm GRP fit a rod-to-stand off fitting to one end and a sail-to-stand off to the other. Attach this to the hole you made in the reinforced dacron on the trailing edge. Insert the top cross spreader (43.5 cm/17.125 in carbon rod) into the two upper leading edge connectors and the two bottom cross spreaders into the lower leading edge connectors and the T-piece. Attach the stand offs to the bottom cross spreaders. The stand offs should be slightly curved.

10 **Making the Bridle:** Follow the same instructions as in Design 1 for 'Pump' for the bridle, but use the following measurements: LONG LINE – 188 cm (74 in) with marks 45 cm (17.5 in) from cut ends; OUTHAUL LINE – 51 cm (20 in) from end of the loop (lark's head knot around leading edge) to knot with 4 cm (1.5 in) loop on end.

Design 3: Tranquillizer

Skill level to make:
Intermediate–Advanced
Skill level to fly:
Intermediate–Advanced
Wind range: 0–16 kph/0–10 mph
0–2 Beaufort scale
Or: **8–32 kph/5–20 mph**
2–4 Beaufort scale

Cost: £35–45

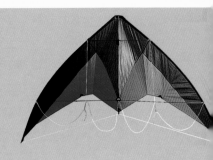

With a 6 mm carbon fibre frame this kite will perform well in no/low wind. With an 8mm carbon frame the maximum increases to 32 kph/20 mph. 'Tranquilizer' will flat spin very easily, stalls are effortless and its axels are slow and predictable. Belly launches, speed control and take-offs are this kite's forte.

Fly on 80–150 lb (36–70 kg) /13.5–33.5 m (40 ft–100 ft) line.

1 **Copy** out the templates from illustration 3.1, using the measurements given, onto the thin card, adding the required seam width (usually 1.5 cm/0.5 in). Cut out each panel, making sure you have noted the marks for leading edge fittings, centre piece and stand off, and especially grain direction.

2 **Cut** out two panels from each template, taking careful note of grain direction. Place the template over the ripstop nylon/polyester, draw around with a soft pencil, then cut out with the craft knife.

3 **Roll** seam the trailing edges of panels B and C (as described in 'General Information'). After sewing the trailing edges of panels B and C, sew the panels together using a roll seam towards panel C. Next sew panel A to B, starting at the the end furthest from the tip and roll seam towards panel A. Close to the tip the roll

YOU WILL NEED:

- Sheet of thin card for template
- 3 m² (3 yd²) ripstop nylon/polyester
- sewing machine and polyester thread
- soft pencil
- ruler
- craft knife
- cutting surface

- 5 cm x 5.5 m (2 in x 5.5 yd) dacron
- 20 cm (8 in) webbing
- 50 cm (20 in) bunji
- 1 x 93 cm (36.5 in) 6 mm carbon rod
- 2 x 165 cm (65 in) 6 mm carbon rod
- 2 x 82.5 cm (32.5 in) 6 mm carbon rod

- 1 x 57 cm (22.5 in) 6 mm carbon rod
- 2 x 25 cm (10 in) 3 mm GRP rod
- soldering iron
- hacksaw
- superglue
- 3 x 6 mm arrow nocks
- 3 x 6 mm end caps

- 4 x 6 mm leading edge connectors
- 6 x 6 T-piece connector
- 2 x 6–3 mm stand off-to-sail fittings
- 2 x 3–6 mm sail-to-stand off fittings
- 3 x 6 mm stoppers
- 100 lb (45 kg) dacron/polyester line

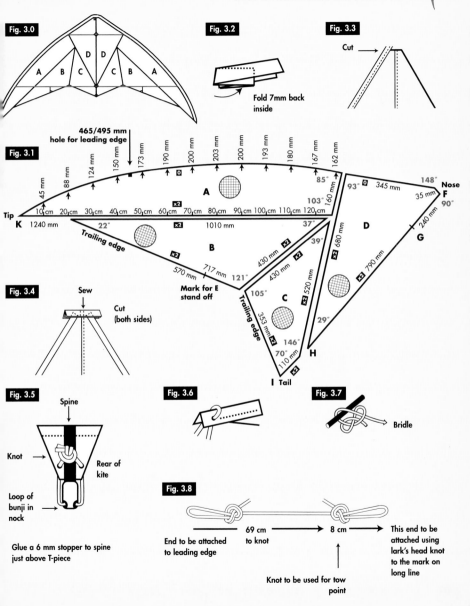

Fig. 3.0

D D
A B C C B A

Fig. 3.2

Fold 7mm back
inside

Fig. 3.3

Cut

Fig. 3.1

465/495 mm
hole for leading edge

45 mm · 88 mm · 124 mm · 150 mm · 173 mm · 190 mm · 200 mm · 203 mm · 200 mm · 193 mm · 180 mm · 167 mm · 162 mm

10 cm 20 cm 30 cm 40 cm 50 cm 60 cm 70 cm 80 cm 90 cm 100 cm 110 cm 120 cm

A

Tip
K 1240 mm

22°
Trailing edge

x2

x2

x2

B

570 mm 717 mm 121°

Mark for E
stand off

85°

103°

160 mm

37°

39°

105°

430 mm

430 mm

x2

x2

520 mm x2

353 mm x2

C

146°

70°

110 mm

I Tail

x2

29°

H

93° 0 345 mm

Nose
F

35 mm

90°

240 mm

G

680 mm

D

790 mm

x2

148°

1010 mm

Fig. 3.4

Sew

Cut
(both sides)

Fig. 3.5

Spine

Knot

Rear of
kite

Loop of
bunji in
nock

Glue a 6 mm stopper to spine
just above T-piece

Fig. 3.6

Fig. 3.7

Bridle

Fig. 3.8

End to be attached
to leading edge

69 cm
to knot

8 cm

Knot to be used for tow
point

This end to be
attached using
lark's head knot
to the mark on
long line

seam will become a trailing edge seam. Finally sew panel D to panels A and C rolling the seam towards panel D. Repeat for the other half of the sail.

4 **Sew** both halves together with a roll seam down the spine. Then sew one continuous additional line around the entire trailing edge.

5 **Cut** seven squares of dacron each 5 cm x 5 cm (2 in x 2 in). Fold one square in half diagonally. At E sandwich the trailing edge in the folded square. Butt the trailing edge up to the diagonal fold in the square so that you have dacron triangles on both the face and back of the sail. Sew through the dacron triangles – reinforcing the point at which the stand off fits. Repeat for the other half of the sail. Then reinforce the tail by sewing dacron squares to the face and the back of the tail – two edges of each square fitting neatly in line with the trailing edges of the tail. Next sew a square of dacron at F (240 mm/19.5 in from the nose). Fold the dacron square in half diagonally, open it and position it so the fold line follows the line of the spine seam. Sew just inside the edges of the dacron square. To reinforce the T-piece area (H), sew two squares of dacron onto either side of the sail as follows: fold the squares in half diagonally, then open them out. Position them 790 mm (31 in) from the nose so the fold follows the line of the spine seam again. Then sew the squares in place.

6 **Cut** a length of dacron 175 cm (69 in) long and fold in half lengthwise. At one end fold the dacron, 7 cm (2.75 in) down, inside itself (see figure 3.2). Sew the leading edge pocket on, following the description given in the instructions for 'Sushi' (Design 2/step 6). Then cut the excess dacron off the nose 790 mm (31 in) from the T-piece reinforcing dacron. Repeat this step for the other wing (see figure 3.3).

7 **Cut** 20 cm (8 in) of webbing and dacron and sew to one an other using a lengthwise central fold as guide. Then fold down the newly sewn line and place across the nose of the kite (see diagram 3.4). Fix this reinforcement sewing around the end caps of spine and both leading edges, taking your time and keeping the fabric taut.

8 **Trim** excess off nose and seal with soldering iron, as with 'Sushi'. Make holes in the following places with

the soldering iron: at each tip (5 cm from the end of dacron leading edge strip) the stand off holes in dacron (E), cut and seal a hole in the T-piece (H), make hole in dacron in tail of spine (I). Make cut outs for the leading edge connectors in the dacron at points K and J. Repeat for the other wing.

9 **Insert** the rods into the sail. The 93 cm (36.5 in) rod forms the spine. Fix the T-piece onto the spine through the sail at point H, so that the connector is on the face and the rod on the back of the kite. Fit a 6 mm end cap on the end that fits in the nose webbing socket, and a 6 mm nock onto the tail end. Cut 15 cm (6 in) of bunji cord and tie it into the holes made in the tail – following instructions given in 'Sushi' (see figure 3.5). Cut the remaining 35 cm (13.75 in) of bunji in half. Tie each piece into the holes at the tips as per figure 3.6. Insert the leading edge rods (165 cm/65 in carbon rods) into the leading edge dacron pockets. Put the leading edge fittings at the cut-out points and an end cap on the end to go into the nose pocket. Fix a 6 mm nock on the tip end. Tension the bunji over the nock as tight as possible so that the sail takes on its characteristic curve. Make two stand offs from the 25 cm (10 in) GRP rods. Attach a sail-to-stand off connector to one end and a stand off-to-sail connector to the other end of each length of GRP. Fit the stand offs into the hole made in the stand off reinforcing dacron on each sail. Insert the top cross spreader (57 cm/22.5 in carbon rod) into the two upper leading edge fittings. Glue a 6 mm stopper just below each top leading edge fitting. Insert the bottom cross spreaders (82.5 cm/32.5 in carbon rod) into the lower leading edge fittings (at K) and into the T-piece connector. Clip the stand offs onto the rods to tension the sail.

10 **Making the Bridle:** This design has a Turbo/ Dynamic set up. Measure and cut a length of 100 lb/45 kg line, 271 cm/106.75 in in length and place marks 61.5 cm/24.25 in from each end. Using a lark's head knot attach this long length of bridle line to the spine just below the T-piece. Tie the ends of the long line to the upper leading edges – between the stoppers and the connectors. Use the knot described in figure 3.7. Next make two outhaul bridle lines (a loop at one end and two knots at the other (*see* figure 3.8). Using a lark's head knot attach the loop to the leading edge, just below the lower leading edge fitting (H). Using another lark's head knot affix the 'mark' made earlier to the first end

knot on the outhaul line. Make two equal sized loops and using a lark's head knot attach them to the second knots in the outhaul bridle lines 8 cm (3 in) along. Attach your flying lines to these two loops just fitted.

Design 4: Flash

Skill level to make:
Beginner/Intermediate
Skill level to fly: Advanced
Wind range: 8–40 kph/5–25 kph
                 2–5 Beaufort scale

Cost: £35

YOU WILL NEED:

- Sheet of thin card for template
- 3 m² (3 yd²) ripstop nylon/polyester
- sewing machine and

- polyester thread
- soft pencil
- ruler
- craft knife
- cutting surface

- soldering iron
- 6 x 8 mm end caps
- 2 x 76 cm (30 in), 8 mm carbon rods
- 2 x 180 cm (71 in),

- 8 mm carbon rods
- 2 x 8 mm arrow nocks
- 50 cm (20 in) of bungie
- 100 lb (45 kg) bridle line

Forget everything you know about two line kite flying – this quad-line kite will challenge your hand-eye coordination! Flash will hover motionless just above the ground, perform lightning fast propeller spins, fly sideways, upside-down and execute dramatic stops. Flash needs between 8–40 kph (5–25 mph/2–5 on the Beaufort scale) of wind.

Fly on a 100 lb (45 kg) line at a length of 22 m (75 ft).

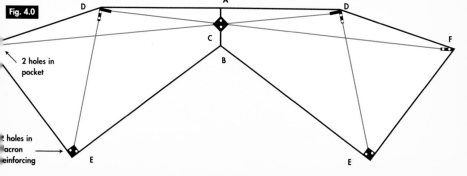

Fig. 4.0

2 holes in pocket

holes in acron einforcing

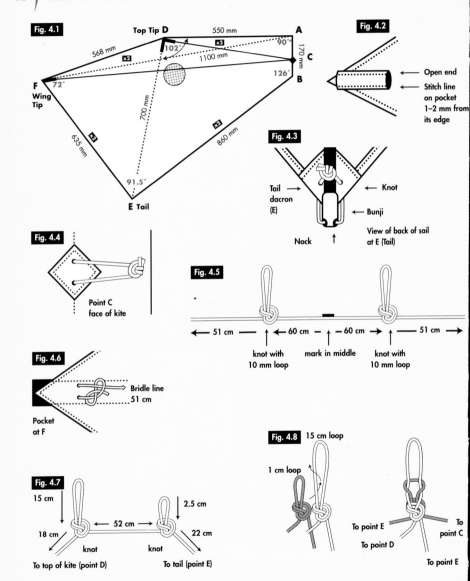

Fig. 4.1

Top Tip D — 550 mm — A

568 mm x2 102° 90°

1100 mm 170 mm C

F 72° 126° B Wing Tip

700 mm

635 mm x2 860 mm x2

91.5°

E Tail

Fig. 4.2

← Open end

← Stitch line on pocket 1–2 mm from its edge

Fig. 4.3

Tail dacron (E) → ← Knot

← Bunji

Nock ↑

View of back of sail at E (Tail)

Fig. 4.4

Point C face of kite

Fig. 4.5

← 51 cm → ← 60 cm → ← 60 cm → ← 51 cm →

knot with 10 mm loop mark in middle knot with 10 mm loop

Fig. 4.6

→ Bridle line 51 cm

Pocket at F

Fig. 4.7

15 cm ↓

18 cm ↙ ← 52 cm → 2.5 cm

knot knot 22 cm ↘

To top of kite (point D) To tail (point E)

Fig. 4.8 15 cm loop

1 cm loop

To point E To point C

To point D

To point E

1 **Using** the thin card, draw and cut out the template, adding 1.5 cm (0.5 in) for the seam allowance around all five sides.

2 **Draw** around the card template onto ripstop nylon/polyester and cut out, repeating this step to make two panels. Pay particular attention to the grain direction. On the fabric panels, draw the positions of the three dacron pockets, following figure 4.1.

3 **Roll** a seam around the whole trailing edge, except the seam between points A and B. Sew the two panels together using a roll/double seam from points F to B, forming a symmetrical kite sail.

4 **Cut** six squares of dacron (5 cm x 5 cm/2 in x 2 in). Position one on the face of the kite at point C and one on the back, again at point C. Sew through both squares securing the dacron, but also sandwiching the kite between, to make a reinforcement point for the bridle. To reinforce the tail, position two dacron squares at point E, one on the face and the other on the back of the sail. Sew them to the sail, and repeat for the opposite wing.

5 **Make** six pockets to be sewn to points D and F. To make a pocket, cut a 10 cm (4 in) strip of dacron 5 cm (2 in) wide. Fold this strip in half lengthwise, then crosswise to make a rectangle of dacron 2.5 cm x 5 cm (1 in x 2 in). Position one pocket at point F, making sure the closed end of the dacron pocket is towards the trailing edge of the sail and the open end towards point C. Sew two lines of stitching 1–2 mm from the longest edges of the pocket as in figure 4.2. Position two dacron pockets at point D, one pointing towards point E and the other pointing towards point C. Sew in place using two stitch lines on each pocket, again 1–2 mm inside the longest edges of the pockets. Repeat this stage for the opposite wing, so you have six pockets overall on the back of the kite.

6 **Using** a soldering iron make seven pairs of holes in the dacron pockets and reinforcing points at the points illustrated in figure 4.3.

7 **Take** one length of 8 mm carbon rod, 180 cm (71 in) long, and put an 8 mm end cap on each end. Slide one end into the dacron pocket at point F and then flex the rod to fit into the pocket at point D on the opposite wing. Repeat with the second 180 cm (71 in) carbon rod in the opposite direction. The two rods should cross at point C. Cut the 50 cm (20 in) bunji in half. Take one length and thread the ends through the two holes on the face of the kite at point E. Tie in a knot and then insert a spine rod. Use a 76 cm (30 in) carbon rod as a spine. Fit an 8 mm end cap to one end and slide the rod into the vertical pocket at point D. Fix an 8 mm arrow nock to the tail end of the spine rod and position the bunji around the nock as described in diagram 4.3. Repeat for the opposite wing.

8 **The Bridle** (attached to the face of the kite). Cut a piece of 100 lb (45 kg) line 22 cm (8.75 in) long. Thread the line through the two holes on the face of the sail at point C, around the rods crossing on the back and tie in a loop (see figure 4.4). Next make a length of line with two 1 cm (0.5 in) loops and a mark in the middle (see figure 4.5). Using a lark's head knot attach this line at its marked middle to the loop of line made at point C. Tie one end of the bridle line, using the two holes, at point F with the knot described in figure 4.6. Repeat for the other side of the kite using the other half of the bridle line.

9 **For** the second bridle line, make a length of line with two loops according to the measurements in figure 4.7. Tie the 'top end' of this bridle line into the two holes made in the dacron pocket at D using the knot in figure 4.6, then tie the tail end of this bridle line, using the same knot, to the holes in the reinforcing dacron at the tail, or E. Next, using a lark's head knot attach the large 15 cm (6 in) loop to the 1 cm (0.5 in) loop of the first bridle line as in figure 4.8. Repeat this step for the opposite wing.

10 **Setting up Your Flying Lines:** Attach four equal-length lines (150 lb/45 kg break strain) to the bridle. Your lines should be around 22 m (75 ft) long. Use a pair of Revolution I ('Rev One') handles. Attach top left line to top left handle and bottom left line to bottom left handle. Repeat for right-hand side. Learn to fly in an 13 kph/8 mph (2 on the Beaufort scale) wind.

Trouble-shooting and Bridle Adjustment

The most obvious kind of problem you can have is breaking a rod. There's nothing you can do about it – everybody, including experts, breaks rods. They're usually not expensive to replace and don't take long to fit. Making repairs is a good way of familiarizing yourself with your kite. Carrying a few spare rods is a good idea, and these should include the spine, lower leading edge and stand off.

Occasionally you might make a hole in your sail with a rod, either by slipping when putting the kite together or if a rod pops out in a heavy crash. Small holes can be repaired quite easily with some sticky-backed nylon repair tape – found in your local kite store. A patch stuck on both sides which is slightly bigger than the hole itself should stop the hole enlarging. Larger tears should be sewn. Most kite shops will do repairs quite cheaply, but all you need is a good domestic sewing machine to be able to do your own. If the spine goes through the nose after repeated crashing, you can darn the hole by hand or sew a new nose on. Small dacron reinforcers (typically at the centre of the kite or where the stand off meets the sail) can be replaced easily. Only really serious damage renders a kite irreparable.

Ongoing care and maintenance of your kite will help keep it flying well. You will find that there's a collar or stopper just below all the leading edge connectors to stop the kite deforming in flight. Check them every now and then and glue any that have come adrift back into place. Also, have a look at the bunjies/elastic/rubber bands at the wing and spine tips. They stretch with time and should be re-tied or replaced to keep them at the correct tension.

Bridle Adjustment

The bridle, or harness, is the string cradle on the front of the kite that you attach your lines to. Most now have a short, doubled length of string with a knot on the end for you to attach your lines to. If not, there will be an aluminium ring or a clip. This is called the tow-point or bridling-point and sets the angle of attack of the kite against the wind. Most bridles have three 'legs' coming to one point, this is called a standard three-point bridle. A dynamic bridle has been developed for trick kites. This type of bridle allows for natural instability, which is very good for radical trick manoeuvres, but not so good for snappy square cornered precision flying. The two different bridle set-ups are shown in the illustration on the right.

Most kites come from the manufacturer with the bridle already in place and pre-set in a position where the kite will fly easily. There's usually a mark on the bridle to show where this point is.

Making adjustments to the bridle will do one of two things: extend your kite's wind range by helping it fly better in either lighter or stronger winds or make the kite handle differently in the same wind. Even on a big wing very small adjustments make a radical difference to the kite, 5 mm–1 cm (0.25–0.5 in) at a time. The smaller the kite the finer the tuning. Generally speaking you will want to bring the nose slightly forwards in either a strong or a light wind. Loosen the knot at the tow point and move the tow point slightly up the top bridle leg then pull the knot tight again. Do the same to both sides. In a strong wind this spills the wind slightly and decreases the pull. In a light wind it helps the kite translate what wind there is into lift. Make sure you adjust back to the original position when the wind is back to a good average. Bringing the nose forward, therefore, makes the kite faster, have less pull and have a less sharp turn. Dropping the nose backwards makes the kite slower, increases the pull and makes turns tighter and crisper. Going too far in either direction will stop the kite flying at all.

With the dynamic or 'turbo' bridle the adjustment is more complex as there are two possible adjustment points. The fine tuning is more sensitive. At the outer adjustment you can move up (towards the nose) which will help the kite fly in lighter winds by generating more lift. It makes the kite faster and turns less tight. Moving down (towards the tip) will help fly in stronger winds and give tighter, more aggressive turns – it slows the kite down and makes it stall more easily. At the inner adjustment you can move in, towards the spine, giving tighter turns but also a tendency to spin. Moving out makes the kite turn wider and helps stability.

With any bridle adjustment be careful, don't overdo it and if you get in a hopeless mess you can always go back to the original settings (where the kite should fly) and start again. If you're in any doubt about it go back to the shop where you bought the kite and consult them. Failing that, contact the manufacturer.

The diagram shows the two different bridle options: on the right is the three-point bridle, which is on most entry level and big wing deltas. On the left is the dynamic bridle, found on many trick and free-style kites. The dynamic bridle is preferred by many, though for a beginner any advantages will be offset by the kite's increased instability.

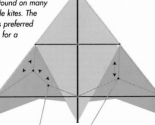